To Mom and Dad who were always there, always. Without your guidance, unconditional love and encouragement, I'd have been lost. You made me the woman I am today (like it or not.)

For my husband, the best man I know. My hero, my funny guy, my rock. The man who takes every challenge MS presents with a "you don't get to win today" attitude. Thank you for waking up every day, seeking out the positive and teaching the rest of us how to savor every priceless moment.

Acknowledgements

Thanks to all the whacky, wonderful real-life characters in this book who bring joy and chaos to the world. I've changed your names but you know who you are! You all mean the world to me and I'm a better person for knowing you.

Foreward

Everyone has a story. It's true. Some are sad stories of hardship and tragedy , while others are full of laughter and joy. I've been transfixed by tales of travel to the farthest reaches of the globe, or daring adventures of skydiving, bunji jumps and scuba diving (nothing, by the way I would EVER try- these people are nuts. Who jumps out of a perfectly good airplane?)

 I've read about mammoth acts kindness and courage that renew my faith in mankind, and been bored senseless by a neighbor who has chosen me as the sounding board for their inane anecdotes.

So you see- good, bad or boring- everyone has a story.

Mindy's musings is a collection of my real life experiences stemming from every day encounters with family, friends and colleagues. These seemingly mundane events are anything but. You'll meet Mom, a leading competitor and favorite in the Jewish Mother Olympics . Her best friends, Food and Worry, make frequent appearances, as do a host of characters who will make you scratch your head, laugh or really feel good about your own situation.

As you thumb through the pages of what I refer to as my "escapades through the extraordinarily ordinary", you'll learn how I to use humor to combat fear, anxiety and a myriad of other challenges. Lessons of how to handle Mom's false arrest at TJ MAXX and coping with party disasters will be bestowed upon you. Finally, this digest of the daily dilemmas that result from both voluntary and involuntary human interaction is chalk full of priceless nuggets that are sure to remind you of someone you know- maybe even yourself!

My hope in sharing my stories is to bring a little laughter to a lot of people. For my family, humor is the ultimate medicine for any ailment- physical or emotional- and is just plain good for you. It's gotten us through hard times, let us take ourselves less seriously and certainly added years and quality to our lives.

So sit back, curl up with a nice cup of coffee or some xanax, and read on!

Mindy

Contents

Chapter One

Living Levy – Meet The Family

Before I introduce you to my family, I want to provide a little background on me. After all, this book, albeit non-fiction, is written 100% from my perspective. It's not uncommon for my family to recount these very stories with a completely different spin. The facts remain, but editorial license is subjective and one person's hero is another's villain.

This chapter will either be abundantly helpful for you to really "get" the humor in these stories, or it will serve to completely confuse and confound you. Good luck either way.

Meet Mindy

I'll keep it brief and to the point. In a nutshell, I worry. I'm a worrier. If you ask any of my friends, family or even the random acquaintance to describe me in one word it will be "worry." The second word would be "kind", and that makes me proud, but worry trumps kind in this contest.

I have all the anxiety naturally attributed to Jewish women and then some. I worry about the food supply, world peace and global warming. I ponder politics, pollution and the world we are leaving to our kids. Will the plane arrive on time, have we packed the right clothes, do the kids need snacks??? And the dog- how do we conquer her thunderstorm phobia? She is going to have a seizure!

All of these things are unwelcome distractions in my vie quotidienne, my daily life. Ever heard the saying, "it is what it is?" That is the dumbest fucking expression ever uttered from the lips of an intelligent being. The question is, WHY is it what it is, what is it going to do to us, and how the hell do we change it?

When I'm not busy confronting such fears, sometimes even while I'm busy confronting this stuff, I have full life with an incredible husband, two step daughters who light up my life, a busy career and more. I enjoy exercise of any kind, inside or out, cooking and learning foreign languages. Travel is a passion as is giving back. I feel tremendously lucky to have had unconditional love from wonderful parents growing up. It's not a given and I'll never take it for granted.

Somehow I want to make a difference and help people. The family is active in multiple charities and volunteer organizations. I'm happiest when I'm with my family doing good for someone in need. My propensity for worry is boundless, but my love for my family is bigger.

That's me today. Let's take a little trip down memory lane and meet the childhood me and my family.

****

Backtrack to suburban Boston, circa 1970's – 1980's. The Levy family-Mom, Dad, Sara, Mindy, Rocky the dog and Kiki the cat- happily cohabitating in domestic harmony sans conflict, drama or discord. Not entirely accurate. Like most nuclear families, we had our fair share of arguments, debates, groundings, battles of wits, etc. But we also shared unconditional love and support for one another that shines on today. It is in the spirit of that unconditional love that I know my family will forgive my very candid account of our lives, maybe even embrace it.

Just to be safe, I've changed the names to protect...well, me.

Dad: Nate Levy. Handsome, funny and intelligent. Majored in romance languages in grad school, no-one knows why, but he ended up in business without speaking a lick of anything but English. My dad was one of the most well-loved people I've ever known. It's true. People gravitated to him like flies to honey. Always the life of the party, always willing to help a friend, the best dad ever.

And completely oblivious.

Dad was a successful career executive, great dad, sage purveyor of advice, and at a complete loss as to how Mom ran the house, managed the kids, pets and career without missing a beat.

More on this later, but suffice it to say that it's only now that I'm a wife, parent and female executive myself, that I recognize how maddening it must have been for my mom. Imagine the never ending dialogue that went something like this between my sister and I: "Dad's so cute. Really. He never gets made unless it's really bad. But Mom, jeesh, she is wound *tight*."

I guess Mom really was justified in hurling a 15 lb chicken across our kitchen floor when Dad tried to cook it at 200 degrees and couldn't understand why it was still raw after 3 hours. We later dubbed the episode "chicken bowling" and fortunately, it has not become a Levy family tradition.

Mom: Blanch Wolbarst Levy. Only child born on the outskirts of Boston, married Nate at age 21. Always independent, Mom was an elementary school teacher turned bank teller turned personnel manager turned executive vice president.

She took great care of the family and balanced career, family and all of the other demands on women back then with no cell phone, PC or ipad at her disposal. Mom is the most generous and supportive people on the planet. She is THE person you want in your corner in times of crisis or worry, or to celebrate your successes and comfort you when you fail.

Unless you are 40 years old playing in a competitive tennis league. Yep, that was me a few years ago. I called Mom from the car after a grueling three hour singles match. I didn't win, but man did I play well! I was stoked, some of my best tennis ever.

Mindy: "Hi, it's me. Yes, just finished the match. No, didn't win but played sooo well. Huh? Yeah, I did play the best I could."

So like all supportive moms, she said it's not if you win or lose, it's if you did your best, right? Wrong.

Mom: "But you didn't win? Why didn't you win? Mindy, you've shamed the family. Call me back when you win."

True story. She was, of course, kidding and we had a laugh. But that's the thing with Mom. You never, ever know what to expect.

Add OCD, type A and a bit of a control freak to the generosity, great sense of humor and sarcasm and that's mom.

Sara and Me: 14 months my senior, Sara and I share the exact same value system. As we age, we are creepily starting to look more and more like one another. That's where the similarity ends. None, zero, zippo, nada, zilch. Sara is a fearless, accident prone, risk taker who will tell you and the rest of the world exactly what she thinks. I am a risk-averse, anxiety prone pleaser who is just finding her path to letting go a bit.

Unwittingly, Sara summed up our situation with the following statement. Allow me to frame it in an analogy. In the giant massage of life (that's my contribution), "You are the rubber and I am the rubbee."

Sara is kind, sweet and the best sister on earth. I'm pretty sure I'm the same to her. While we are polar opposites, we are as close as two siblings can be. She is my rock, my friend and the crazy, fun-loving alter ego I hope to someday embrace myself. If you combine us, we make a hell of a whole person!

So that's the garden from which I sprouted. We had good soil and our roots run deep. Now that you know the family, let's dive into what I refer to as my daily escapes into the extraordinarily ordinary. Living Levy- just like your family. But different.

Chapter Two:

The "F" Words: Food and Family

Two themes recur throughout the book: food and family. While in no particular order, these entwined elements set the stage for the adventure on which you are about embark with me- hope you enjoy the ride.

Food For Thought

Jewish people love food. Our world revolves around food. Before we finish breakfast we've decided what's for lunch. Passover, important holiday, great food. Yom Kippur, NO food, but a break fast that rivals Thanksgiving. Bar-Mitzvahs and weddings- food fantasies. Food is THE deciding factor of a successful or failed vacation. Was the food good? Was it too expensive? Was there enough of it???

Oh, and don't forget the service. The food was exceptional but that waiter, he destroyed our entire dining experience thereby ruining a perfectly planned vacation. Didn't he know the precious cargo he transports from kitchen to consumer is like life support for a cardiac patient??? OY

Restaurants, for my family, are the source of countless happy memories, awkward exchanges, sudden and angry departures, political and emotional disputes, and inappropriate behavior. What better venue? A restaurant serves as the perfect tribunal from which the defendant cannot escape. She is captive. Especially if she arrived at court in the same vehicle as judge and jury (i.e. Mom, Dad and the occasional guest jurors, willing siblings.

Happy memories are by far the winner of all my restaurant experiences in both volume and variety. It would be a gross disappointment, virtually unacceptable, for any self-respecting Jewish woman to have less than a lifetime of funny, tears rolling down your face stories from across the tablecloth restaurant mishigas.

Mommom At The Chinese Restaurant

Chinese food. We loved Chinese food and frequented some fab restaurants growing up. My dad's mom, Mommom, was also a big Chinese food fan. She was one of my favorite people in the entire world. We were extremely close (though we had our moments when I was a kid) and I miss her every day since she passed away at 97 a few years ago.

Known for a "healthy" appetite, Mommom started every meal with, "I'm not very hungry." Later in life I came to learn that this is code for "I am starving and will clear my plate and yours if you let me." Mom would whisper, "Watch, she's going to say it" in my ear and we'd laugh. Sure enough, there it was. Then we'd order extra spare ribs and fried rice, just in case wink, wink.

Then one time at the Chinese restaurant the earth stopped. Wait for it. Wait for it. It's coming. Then, nothing. She said nothing. Holy shit, she really was hungry? Or was she sick? Should we call someone? Who? Was it a ploy and she was faking us out? We were completely confused, unable to decipher what was happening. Do we order more food? Do we order less food? It was horrible. Mom was pinching me under the table, I was disoriented and we just banded together to get through it.

We opted out of extra ribs and rice and decided to just move on. Good conversation, updates on school and friends, my sister looking like she would rather poke fork in her own eye than be with us and my dad, quiet as always.

The food came, yum! Just the right things and just enough. Then the lights dimmed, other patrons went silent, somewhere church bells were chiming (ok, that last one was for effect.). All eyes were on Mommom. No! This can't be. Timing is all wrong. The food is ON the table. Nooooooo.

Yes.

"I'm really not very hungry."

****

Mom vs. The Maître D'

After you read this, you'll understand more about our family restaurant dynamics.

We did not grow up poor. Not rich, but a happy middle class family with a full set of silverware in our kitchen. I share this tidbit because my mother could not leave a restaurant without a small token of our visit. My dad referred to this as stealing. My mom begged to differ, after all, no-one would miss a tiny olive dish or butter knife. Fortunately, purses in the 80's and 90's were small suitcases.

Like hockey to Canadians and soccer to our friends in Europe, scoring just the right item from the table was competitive sport to my mother. I'll use the ubiquitous football analogy here. Butter knife- first down. Salt and pepper shakers- field goal. Coffee creamer with the most adorable handle ever- TOUCHDOWN. Made my dad nuts. I thought it was funny and have to admit to this day I have a few unmatched items in my own fork drawer.

****

To Tell The Truth- Not The Game Show

This is not about the classic game show in which a person of some notoriety and two impostors try to match wits with a panel of four celebrities. It's about something much more serious.

Can't avoid it. ***Death.***

Just kidding, I'm not feeling morose today. While it's true, you can't avoid death, I'm writing about something else because death is yet another fear that plagues me and requires, deserves actually, much more airtime than a mere mention in the "Food" chapter . Remember this about me? "I'm a worrier. I have all the anxiety naturally attributed to Jewish women and then some." We'll have *loads* of time to focus on worry... and death.

Right now I want to further explore the whole Jewish/Food connection. Talk about an enmeshed relationship!

Let's jump back in the time machine and go back to 1986. My sister's 21st birthday dinner. Imagine a house bustling with excitement for the big night out. Toto or Dream Academy on the radio.   Let the celebration begin.....

Hair moussed to perfection, blue eye shadow from lid to brow and shoulder pads securely velcroed inside our multi-colored sweaters (1980's), Mom, my sister and I descend the stairs of our split level suburban Boston home where Dad waits. And waits. And waits.

G-D forbid we leave on our first try. I may be biased, as I recount everything in this book from my own experience and perspective, but it was never me who had a debilitating hair catastrophe, spilled my purse, broke up with my boyfriend, tore my dress or had a random emotional breakdown that prevented a simple departure for dinner. That would be Sarah, my sister.

Today we refer to her as high maintenance. She's had many years to perfect and live up to this label and the only qualified rival is my mother.

Anyway, back to the birthday dinner. We did eventually get to the restaurant. You'll recall that this is the big 21 celebration. Yep, first time she can legally drink with Mom and Dad. FYI, alcohol, parents and new found independence, not a good combo.

Don't panic, the food was great! Phew. We had a wonderful meal, lots of laughing and love all around. Presents and all eyes on my sister, the way she likes it.

Then it happened.

For some reason unbeknownst to me, maybe the three bottles of wine, Sarah decided it was time to enlighten my parents about how she had spent her leisure time through high school and college. Parties while they were out of town, yeah they knew. At least she started small and eased them into what was coming.

The boyfriend (yeah, the one with her name tattooed on his forearm with whom she got arrested for possession of marijuana, *him*.) Well, she kinda saw him for two more years until *she* decided it was time to call it off. Had he been in our house? "Sure, but only when you guys were out of town." Nice.

Then there was the time she cracked up the car. She came home and told my mom she hit a fire hydrant. Being the ever-trusting, normal parent that my mother was and is, she made Sarah go back out in the car with her to see the offending fire hydrant for herself. Of course there was no fire hydrant, Sarah had been out with aforementioned, banned bad boy. We got a laugh out of the two hour fire hydrant scavenger hunt they went on, until my sister broke like a vase on a cement floor. Grounded. Again.

We shared loads of stories, mostly hers, and all had to dry the tears from laughter from our cheeks. Mission accomplished.

Until they proudly announced how funny and colorful my sister is. I, apparently, am dull, uninteresting and overall nice but pretty boring. I think they actually used a reference to the color beige.

Really? Really? I was on the tennis team, had a great group of friends (were they beige, too?), active social life and was a pretty easy going, happy kid. Beige? I'll show you.

"So by the way, you DO know that aforementioned, banned bad boy was the first boy Sarah slept with, right?" Dad, chalk white. Mom, glaring. Sister, fuming.

I'll show you beige.

****

There Were No Jews On The Food Committee

One of Kevin's work friends was having a surprise 50th birthday party for his wife. I didn't know them very well (sort of not at all) but we'd been invited to a few of their get-togethers over the years and hadn't made any of them. I was overseas traveling when Kevin told me about the invitation and asked if I wanted to go. Being the hard core, stayupallnight party animal that I am (*not*), I said, "sure, sounds fun." We like parties, we're pretty likeable ourselves and it's always fun to meet new people.

Aside: Kevin told me over dinner recently that he thought we should be going out more, you know, diversifying our "friend portfolio". We have tons (like I said, we're pretty likeable) but tend to spend most of our time with Jan and Jay, our besties. Lately they've been talking about moving and Kevin thinks we're going to become the Lonely Levy Cat People if we're not careful. Thus my quick "let's go to the surprise party for people I don't know" response.

Anyway. Kevin tells me the party is in a couple of weeks and he rsvp's that we'll be there. What Kevin doesn't tell me is the party is a 'Cruising to 50' theme and we are to don "cruise wear" and all guests are to bring an appetizer. Oh and don't park at the house (obviously- note "surprise" in the party title) but drop your appetizer off and park your car in the nearby park.

The evite came with instructions, too! From 6-7 the cruise departs and we will talk about the birthday girl. From 7-8 the appetizers YOU bring will be available for consumption on the Promenade Deck. We sprung for a cake that you need to eat before 10pm when the cruise ends.

Hang on, hang on- we need to dissect this.

First- define cruise wear. Is this the redneck jumpsuit thingy embellished with gold I've seen on The Love Boat? Is it a skimpy bathing suit? Do I have to see my husband in a very unsexy, Thirston Howell III Captain's hat? We discussed this at length as I have never been, nor have any desire to go, on a cruise. We opted not to dress as Lovey and Thurston and chose a Hawaiian shirt for Kevin and jeans with boat shoes for me.

Second- who invites you to a party and demands you show up with an appetizer to feed the other guests *they* invited? Clearly not a Jewish event. If it's a pot luck, call it pot luck in the invite and be done with it.

I'd go a step further here and recommend they include the following disclaimer on their evite:

"No Jews were involved in the planning of this event. We take no responsibility for guests who dislike the food and/or entertainment. Boredom is a strong possibility. Any reference to "Scrapebook" in the invitation is really a reference to the scrapbook to which you are supposed contribute as part of the free gift we opted for the celebrant vs. a real present. There is a strong possibility you will leave this event hungry, disappointed and tired."

Finally, the parking. You may drop your appetizer off, drive far away from our house in the dark then find your way back after we have secured your Potato Poopies and Corn Curlies. This is a master festivity FAIL.

So how did it turn out, you ask? The party was last night. I was a bit under the weather but pushed forward because I was Kevin's first mate and didn't want to let him down. Sadly, by the time were supposed to leave, I was seasick and we hadn't left port yet. Kevin was a trooper and said he could go solo while I rested at home. He's a keeper (and no, I wasn't faking.) So I packed up the homemade hummus Kevin made with a nice bag of chips, donned my pj's and wrapped up in a blanket with a book.

Just like the evite schedule dictated, Kevin returned from sea around 10:30pm (had to drive from port back to our house.) In his hand was a bag from Taco Bell and a beer. Huh? What happened to the hummus and potato poopies? My hubby has an appetite but is not into the whole fourth meal fad so this was odd.

"There were no Jewish people on the food committee."

Hahahha, my non-Jewish husband summed it all up in one sentence. Although he had to use his iPhone gps to navigate back to the house from the park (and saved a few guests at the same time) he did make it to the party. They did, in fact, talk about the birthday girl, enjoy the scrape book/scrap book and eat cake from a local restaurant.

However, it was a race to the appetizer table and all the good stuff went fast. Some partygoers didn't get much of anything. Kevin scored some olives, shrimp and his own dip. When they said appetizers they meant appetizers…and nothing else!

No sarcasm here but…."Hello, please come to our house for a 5 hour party. Make sure you arrive early and you'll be her till 10 with limited food. Hope you can run faster than Barb and Pete to the table or you're shit out of luck. So be sure to eat a big lunch."

I sat with Kevin while he ate his Taco Bell after party meal. We laughed and I think he was actually relieved that I stayed behind.

Except for the awkward moments where he was petting their dog, alone. He did say he made some friends but it dawned on him, as he took the last bite of that delicious mystery meat taco, that we were likely invited to this party by accident. The friend wrote and sent the invite with the scrape book and appitizer is not a party planner by trade and should have validated the invitation list before hitting send.

****

A Jewish Limerick

This food debacle inspired me, I guess I just couldn't let it go. This limerick came to me while I was walking the dog tonight- no clue why but here you go.

A party was planned cuz she's fifty
The cruise theme was meant to be nifty
The guests all appeared
It was just what they feared
No Jews meant the buffet was thrifty

Or

Her birthday was reason to sail
A cruise theme with presents and ale
The guests all arrived
Some didn't survive
No Jews meant the food was a FAIL

Or

Parties are simply the best
Even when you're the wrong guest
With hummus and chips
A smile on his lips
He realized they should have confessed

****

There ARE Jews On The Food Committee

Tonight Kevin and I are going to a 40th birthday celebration my friend, Kyla. We're really looking forward to it. You'll recall just a short time ago, we were invited to a 50th birthday celebration that was a colossal catering cluster. Tonight promises to be just the opposite. How do I know?

The entire party- food, venue, attendees- planned by Jews.

Enough said. But this is my blog and you expect to read something so I'll continue. Admittedly, these are derivatives of Jewish party planning but they merit the mention.

-No-one was requested or required to bring, well, anything (ie no appetizer required for entry.)

-We can park on the street RIGHT in front of the house vs. a spooky, dark playground down the street. Whoop!

-There is no scheduled time to "talk about the birthday girl" (never been big on "sharing" at parties) We actually have no fucking clue what will happen between 8pm-midnight! Paarrrtyyyy!

-Possibly most important, this party lacks any theme with the exception of happy birthday Kyla. No prerequisite for me to wear "cruise attire" or any other cutesy costume that would undoubtedly spark competition, controversy and the envy of the other party goers because my outfit is the best. Crisis averted!

So there you have it. We can't wait to celebrate Kyla's big day. The sumptuous "heavy appetizers", great company and creative cocktails won't suck either.

Party Preparation

No, not the party *givers*, the party *goers*! The hosts have everything under control (yes, I checked and rechecked and will check again before we leave tonight!)

So how does one prep for this highly anticipated food filled festivity? Well, one could lie like most goyim do before Christmas and say…"I won't eat for days because I know the food is going to be soooo good and there will be soooo much."

But I don't know any Jews that would find ANY reason to skip a meal with the exception of Yom Kippur. And then, we eat for months to amass enough body fat to sustain us for the 24 hours of hell that is our annual repentance. Suffice it to say, we had a good breakfast, an even better lunch and we will not disappoint at the buffet tonight.

Gifts. The host, Kyla's husband, specifically said "no gifts please" on the invite. This is how this is going to go down folks.

Every Jew will arrive with a gift in one hand and wine, champagne or other spirit in the other. It's not that we don't follow directions (ok, most of us don't as evidenced by my mom but we don't have time for *that* issue today.) It's just a thing, it's what we do. We love to celebrate others' happiness and successes. What better way than with food, gifts and wine???

Every non-Jew will arrive with sincere warm wishes, a smile on their face and... empty hands. It's not that they're not kind and generous, they are. But the invitation clearly stated, "no gifts". Oh, they also won't feel any guilt when they see what the tribe has brought (unless, perhaps, they are Catholic.)

Anyway, it's all good. Tonight is about Kyla. So let's get in the party spirit. T-minus two hours until the carousing commences. I'll be sure to post a follow up soon as I know you will be waiting with bated breath to see if my party prediction prevails.

Chapter Three

Mostly Mom

You met Mom briefly in Chapter One. She's quite a character, full of wisdom, kindness, humor and experience. On the flip side, flexibility is not exactly her forte. Adherence to rules doesn't rank high on her priority list either.

The following stories represent some of the funniest- and some of the most challenging- events I can remember with Mom. They illustrate Mom's uncanny ability to defy rules and skirt disaster (just barely.) They reveal some secret tactics that Mom, this "master of mischief", has employed over the years to get a desired outcome from Sara and I. It's only now that I'm in my forties and on "equal ground" with Mom (okay, we're not quite equal, YET) that I have seen the light.

So read on. I'm sure you'll see in your Mom some of the things I share about mine. But just some. Unless your Mom got arrested at TJ MAXX.

Mom To The Maxx!

So I am leaving on a business trip and I get a phone call from my mom. I get these calls because I live in the same city as Mom. In fact, I get all of the calls, arrests, hospitals, errands (and all the good stuff, too) because I have always lived within 20 minutes of my parents. My sister is on the opposite coast. She does however, still carry my mom's AMEX card, send jewelry and purses back east for my parents to fix for her and otherwise depend on them for emotional support. Getting the picture?

Back to the call.

"I'm at TJ Maxx. You need to come here right now. I've been arrested for shoplifting."

Really? Shoplifting? At TJ Maxx? Why not Nordstrom or Macy's? And, does TJ Maxx management have any idea how much coin my mother drops in their store every year? Let me clue you in because I pulled the records before we went to court. Five figures annually. Low five figures, but five figures. Were they singlehandedly trying to drop their stock price down by arresting my mom?

So I race off to TJ Maxx. When I arrive I am met by a police officer. I explain that I am the accused's daughter and that this must be a mistake. My sixty something year old mother has never stolen a thing in her life.

"Well she should not have started now." Excellent, this is going to be fun.

Oh, have I mentioned that my mother is an executive vice president at a sizable organization and has enough money to buy the entire home section of TJ Maxx? Details.

Mom is being held in some super secret back room where she was escorted earlier by the elite TJ Maxx undercover security team. They won't let me in to see her so I take a seat and wait. When she finally emerges, she looks frightened, pale and worn out.

The incident occurred one year to the day after my father passed away. They were married for forty years and it had been a very rough year. We walked out of the store together, court citation in hand.

So what happened? Well, here's the bottom line. My mom did not steal anything. No shocker there. She did, however, in stellar mom fashion, *break the rules*.

Digression: my mother seems to think she is not subject to the same rules as everyone else. This applies to driving, medical care, tableware (reference the earlier *"Mom vs the M'aitre D'"* post) and, of course, returning goods to TJ Maxx without a receipt.

It was a case of mistaken identity. Not really, but I've always wanted to say that. What happened, and was subsequently proven, was that my mother had purchased some picture frames a few days earlier in the same store. I know this to be true because I saw said picture frames at her house the day before. She said she was returning them and had them in a TJ Maxx bag.

When she returned to the store there were several people in the line for customer service/returns. The rule, wait your turn. The other option, go into the store and shop for more stuff with the picture frames safely tucked in the TJ Maxx bag, then make an exchange. The rule, option two is ok if you have a receipt. However, option two promises a world of pain if you do not have a receipt. Mom took option two sans receipt.

Upon checkout, where by the way she was allowed to return the cheap frames for a store credit and spent another hundred bucks, she departed the store.

"Maam, please step back inside the store."

"What?"

"You heard me, back inside. We saw you steal those frames."

It went downhill from there. The undercover security folks took a lot of pleasure arresting an older woman, by herself, in schlumpy clothes and no makeup. I saw them laughing and gloating outside the holding room. WTF?

Fast forward to mom and me in a dingy courtroom with the dregs of society. A month has passed and we know the case will be dropped because she has stalked TJ Maxx's national head of security until he heard her story. In parallel, I had her print he credit card statements for the last year to demonstrate the level of patronage she offers their kind establishment. She fedexed the full story, credit card reports and details of mistreatment to the CEO of TJ Maxx.
After weeks, they apologized and said they were dropping the charges. Unfortunately, our uber efficient court system could not process the information before we spent the day with child support defaulters, traffic and parole violators and a host of other interesting people I would not invite to dinner (again the food thing.)

Moral of the story? I may be a boring, rule-bound, goody-goody, but I follow the rules and don't get arrested. Do you think Mom ever shopped again at TJ Maxx? I'll leave you in suspense. If you really want to know you need to email me at mindysmusings@gmail.com. I'd be happy to update you!

****

Tanning Hazard- And It's Not The UVA/UVB Rays

Speaking of arrests, and still kind of shopping....

Back in the 90's, before my sister moved out west, my mom and sister went tanning together at a local tanning salon. Sometimes Dad would go get a coffee and wait in the lobby for them. On this particular day my mom and sister checked in to wait for their turn in the tanning bed. The twenty something receptionist was indifferent to them. She was, however, quite attentive to her friends who were moved right through to the best tanning beds while my family waited.

My sister decided this was unacceptable and very clearly shared this with miss twenty something. The argument escalated and the manager arrived. Mom and Dad pleaded for her to let it go but by now it was game on. The manager called the police and my mother, father and sister were escorted from the premises. Perhaps the whole TJ Maxx thing makes more sense now.

****

Oh My Oxymoron!

Do bullies get bullied? Do celebrity chefs really NOT like the food they cook? Is there really such a thing as a "working " vacation or is it just really "work"???? I have dozens of these questions as a result of the conversation I just had with my very JEWISH mother who told me she is becoming anti-Semitic after living in Florida.

It's true. She made the pronouncement after a particularly unpleasant trip to Publix in Boynton Beach. Anyone who has spent any time in a real

24

life Del Boca Vista (a la Seinfeld) knows how perilous a simple trip to the market can be. Sure, dealing with loud, entitled, aggressive (oh, and cheap) senior citizens takes its toll, but to declare war on your own tribe? This merits a closer look.

In Defense of the Anti-Semitic Jewish Mom:

The Publix Parking Lot:
Never mind the pushy patrons inside, the parking lot alone presents a plethora of potential hazards to your health. The vast majority of the old people there can't see over the dashboard, are oblivious to their surroundings and, in general, don't give a shit. Maybe they think, "there's not that much time left anyone, so what the fuck, I'll drive the way I want to..." The rose colored glasses side of me prefers to think they are just, well, old. But I've seen it firsthand and am sad to report.... they are mean.

The Flea MarketParking Lot:
So we're at the local flea market. Mom's chatting up a friend who works at the jewelry counter and I'm buying monogrammed bags for the kids. Another quiet day in retirement paradise, right? Wrong.

Sirens, fire trucks and the police. I go flying to the entrance to the flea market. "Lady Down, Lady Down!" Can't anyone hear me?? I said, "Lady Down!" There is a little old lady laying on the pavement right in front of the building. An old guy steps out of his giant car (circa 1980) like he just ran over a curb, not a person. And no-one inside or outside is doing ANYTHING! How can this be???? Am I the only one who can actually SEE this? Are all the people around me not really there and I'm in some kind of Twilight Zone parallel universe?

No- like the people in the Publix parking lot- they don't give a shit. This Flea Market makes Publix look like a cake walk.

The paramedics help the woman to her feet, thank G-d she is ok. The man leaves, fire truck and ambulance depart, and I am left alone, stunned. So I go back inside to the jewelry counter where Mom and her friend are still kibitzing about one thing or another.

"Mom, did you see that? That man just hit that lady. I thought she was dead! Didn't you hear the sirens?" Mom just smiled at her friend who replied, "Happens every day. We hardly ever lose one."

Dunkin Donuts
Mr. Hyman: (really loud after he cuts me in line) "I want a bagel **lightly** toasted with butter. I want coffee, really hot, with extra milk."

Clerk: "Ok, you can pick up your bagel over there. Here's your coffee."

Mr. Hyman: "I said **HOT.** You call this hot?"

I think actually yes, she did call the steaming cup of java hot, but what do I know. Just get out of my way so I can order. He goes to the other counter to pick up his bagel and I place my order. From across the room...

"I said LIGHTLY toasted. This is too dark. Send it back." Really, send it back? At Dunkin Donuts? This is not a breakfast buffet at the Ritz. It's also not a gourmet meal. It's a friggin' bagel.

I go to Dunkin Donuts every morning for my mom and this happens *every* time. Never fails. Sometimes it's the bagel, sometimes it's the coffee, sometimes it's the weather. All I know is it always *something.*

Okay- some legitimate points on the trail to Jewish Mother anti-Semitism. But we need to look at the other side of the equation to accurately assess the claim. After all, one can look out and pass judgment, but one needs to really look IN before officially converting.

Opposition to the Anti-Semitic Jewish Mom:

My argument against the claim is a simple one. Try these on:

-Anyone who utters the words, "Why am I being punished?" when she wakes up is ineligible for anti-Semitism. Check.
-People who respond to a phone call from their daughter with, "Oh, you are alive" are disqualified. Check.

-Ever replied, "I'll make it" to the question "how are you?" BUZZZZzzzzz, thank you for being a contestant in "I want to be a Jewish anti-Semite". Here is your parting gift.

So folks, what do you think? Do we allow her the label or politely decline? You've got my vote… what's yours?

* * * * * * * * * * * * * * * * * * * *

"Your Sister Loves Me More Than You Do"

Wait, wait. Don't jump to the conclusion that Mom is unabashedly employing her (very solid) aptitude in the instilling Jewish guilt arena. This one was something different. Yes, she said it. But you really need context to grasp the insult the resides in the statement. It was NOT that Sara loves her more. Really. Here's how the conversation went.

Mom: "Your sister loves me more than you do. She'd go to jail for me."

Mindy: "I would go to jail for you in a heartbeat!"

Loooooong pause.

"As long as I didn't have to break any rules or do anything wrong to land in jail for you."

Knowing smirk, and not on my face. The hook was set, and I bit.

So, you see. This was not a free ticket to a mother-daughter guilt trip, it was a cleverly masked statement that Sara is a risk-taking, fun-loving person who likes life on the edge and I'm a bland, lackluster scaredy cat that needs to get out more. Well played, Mom. Well played.

* * * * * * * * * * * * * * * * * * * *

"I Can't Process Water"

A Mom classic. Sara and I crack up over this one again and again. It's the gift that just keeps giving.

Mom was sick and the doctor told her to drink a lot of fluids. With Mom you need to be very precise because she will hear only exactly what is said if convenient. On other occasions, the omission is more effective and she'll use what was NOT said on you. Very tricky indeed.

In this case, the doctor should have said, "Mrs. Levy, you must drink a lot of WATER."

Friends and family were stopping by with food, cases of bottled water, flowers. Nice. Mom is loved a lot. Miraculously, after a week, most of the water was still there. Huh? What was going on? Sara called her to find out. Mom's response was ,"I can't process water. My body doesn't like it. "

Rather than fight with her on the spot, she was sick after all, Sara called me.

"You aren't going to believe what she's come up with now! 'She can't process water.'" What the fuck? Who can't process water? Aren't humans made up of like almost all water? What has she been doing all these years? I know this just can't be true. There is water in Pepsi, Coffee and even pasta sauce. She drinks 2 of the first, the second with cream and 4 sugars and loves a bit of the third over angel hair pasta.

That was a few years ago. I am happy to report that Mom now drinks a good 30 ounces of water a day, minimum. We know she only does it when we're around and opts for the Pepsi and Dunkin Donuts java otherwise, but it's progress.

In the meantime, we've added "I can't process water" to the arsenal of Momisms we are amassing.

****

Words With Friends (And Mom!)

We got Mom an iPad II for her birthday a few months ago. We weren't sure how it was going to go but at 71 she is a whiz! She has her music, pictures and email all cranking on her tablet! She also plays Angry Birds and is pretty cut throat with Words With Friends.

I am a huge Words With Friends player. I can't get enough of it! I'm not quite as avid as Alec Baldwin (who I freaking LOVE) but I hold my own.

On my last visit to Florida (remember, she spends the winters there because she is an official snowbird) we were having our usual Dunkin Donuts coffee (yes, cream four sugars for her) and enjoying a quiet morning together. At the kitchen table. Not talking. On dueling iPads, volume muted so as not to distract. We are completely focused on our respective missions to find that 50 point word in Words With Friends.

Not happening for me. Too many vowels. Shit. 14 points. I enter my word and wait. The breakfast room is sunny, quiet, pleasant. I take a sip of my coffee. Yum. I do love a good cup of Dunkin Donuts coffee.

As I wait for Mom's next word, I reflect on the sad fact that I live in a house divided. It saddens me. I've spent years trying to reconcile why my husband hates Dunkin Donuts coffee. But I can't. I mean, what is wrong with him? Starbucks? Yeah, if you like your coffee *burned*! I mentioned this to my best friend in Boston who simply gasped. It was at that moment that I realized I cannot reveal this irreverence to my hometown peeps because he will be forever banned from Boston. So I remain mum and respectfully ask you to do the same.

Back to the game. No ding, just a screen notification. Remember, we're focused, sound muted.

Oh no. I don't dare to look away from my screen. My internal dialogue says, "Don't, Mindy. Do NOT look up." But I can't help myself. It was like a magnet was drawing my eyes to hers. 58 points. She had a 58 point word.

I look up at Mom. Evil grin. Ghastly, really. Everything went into slow motion for me and I hoped it would stay that way so maybe what was coming next would never come. But it didn't stay that way, and what was coming next was worse than I could ever have imaged.

"58 points Mindy. 58 fucking points!!! Yeah!" It think she even threw in another "F-you" at the end, but I was so stunned by the first profane declaration that I don't know. Then she got up and fiddled around the kitchen like nothing happened.

Later that morning I told her that her dropping the F bomb on me really woke me up to some "stuff". It explained a lot (and it wasn't exactly a compliment.) She very proudly replied that yes, in fact, she believes it is her competitive nature that gave me the desire to compete and ability to achieve that has made me the successful career woman I am today.

 "And by the way, honey. Your fourteen point word was a very good one. I love you."

And she does. She loves me.

Chapter Four
Don't Worry, Be Happy

You'll recall from chapter one that I am a worrier. No big deal, right? Lots of folks worry. Parents worry when their teenage children take the car for the first time. Just before a presentation, the presenter may experience anxiety about public speaking. Someone who has lost their job frets about how to make the next mortgage payment. It's a normal, rational response to a stressful situation.

But that's not me. I can do that presentation, cool as a cucumber. We've planned well financially and lived within our means. So when I got laid off a few years ago, it was a nice little break. No sir, my apprehension doesn't stem from cause and effect events. It is ubiquitous. According to the U.S. National Library of Medicine, the medical term is "generalized anxiety disorder", a pattern of frequent, constant worry over a variety of activities and events. And, it's very common (one less thing to worry about- I'm not the only one!)

I've been this way since childhood. Circa 1970, Kindergarten. Gym class? NOOOO way. Not for me. Was it those menacing ropes hanging from the ceiling? Or perhaps Mr. Bell, the 5'1", paunch bellied, badminton racquet wielding gym teacher? Who knows. I did like that game we played with the parachute, but the palpitations caused by field day undid any enjoyment I experienced running under the brightly colored chute from one side to my friends eagerly waiting on the opposite end. (Ironically, I love working out and am in the gym almost every day... go figure.)

As an adult, I've learned to counter this agonizing emotion with humor. It works, really. Most days I can recognize where true worry is warranted versus my personal "dread demon" and we all get a good laugh. I'm not embarrassed by it and have stopped wishing it away. If this is the worst thing I need to overcome in life, well I'm pretty lucky.

And others benefit from it, too. A few years ago I was getting the family ready for a road trip to visit my in-laws. The kids were 6 and 9. Our youngest looked up at me as I was stuffing her backpack and said, "You know what's great?" I smiled and asked her what was great, expecting something on the lines of how much fun our road trips were, or how she couldn't wait to see Gramma and Papa.

"None of us have to worry about anything. You do it all for us. It's great."

Enough said. I'm not out of the twelve step program. Yet.

****

Don't Sweat The Small Stuff

Anxiety, (also called **angst** or **worry**), as defined by Wikipedia, is a psychological and physiological state characterized by somatic, emotional, cognitive, and behavioral components. *It is the displeasing feeling of fear and concern.*

First, what the fuck does "somatic" mean. I am f-r-e-a-k-i-n-g out right now. Is anxiety worse than I really thought? What symptoms have I missed? Are there yet more elements to anxiety that I am not aware of but am likely suffering from? Yes, I know you don't end sentences with a preposition, but if I am in a full out panic from my discovery of this rare, deadly somatic malady thing from which I will likely die, I'll use whatever grammar I please. (Let's see who was astute enough to catch the irony in that last sentence.)

But I digress. I consider myself an intelligent person and, since I had to look it up, I thought maybe you need to know, too. Somatic simply means "of the body" and in medical terms that means "not mental" as in illness. I stopped reading there in case there was further detail of what "of the body" entailed because I spied the word mutation on the page. I didn't want to develop (by power of suggestion) any of the disgusting afflictions or ailments that are considered "of the body."

Second, "It is the displeasing feeling of fear and concern" is to anxiety as dinghy is to the Titanic. The jackass that wrote that description has never, ever had a real, drain the blood from your face and render you paralyzed, panic attack.

So there you have it, the publicly accepted definition of anxiety. Now here's mine:

The inexplicable, unpredictable, irrational physical and emotional "I am going to die a horrible, never seen before type of death RIGHT NOW and no-one can help me" response to..... nothing in particular. It also entails brooding, obsessing and constant attention to the "what might happen" versus a logical cause and effect approach to the risks of daily activities like taking an aspirin (Could I be allergic? Is anaphylactic shock a possibility or just hives if I am, in fact, allergic? Was the package safety sealed? Is it past the expiration date?)

This is my day to day life folks. I said it early on: I'm a worrier. I worry. My friends make fun of me for it, my kids say the don't need to worry about anything because I do it for them but no-one actually complains. You know why? Because if any of these people get stuck on a desert island with me they know they'll have snacks, bottled water and a pretty decent first aid kit- all from my purse. If their pants shrunk or if they lose a button I have the "As Seen On TV... Perfect Fit Button" pants extender that instantly makes your pants fit perfectly. If there is the sniff of a cold (bad pun) I am stocked with a mini pharmacy at all times.

While it is exhausting to worry like this, and I am the brunt of frequent jokes and mockery, I can't stop. It's like crack. I've tried to take my dad's advise over and again: "Don't sweat the small stuff." He was a master of practicing what he preached. He was calm, collected and measured.

Until he got really pissed off. Then it was no holds barred. But until you got there, the small stuff just slid on by.

Anyway, I tried to adhere to my dad's mantra but I couldn't. Worry, it's like crack. I can't get enough. I try to give it up but no amount of rehab can set me free. No twelve step process will save me. No family intervention will unravel the tangled web of worry I've wound over the last 46 years.

What will I do next, you ask? How will I cope with this narcotic called worry? Well, my coping mechanism is humor. Like when I got a spider bite on my butt and told my husband I was in anaphylactic shock because

I couldn't breathe. I dropped my pants in the kitchen and flipped completely out.

My husband quickly pointed out that I was, in fact, breathing because I was talking, taking actual breaths, to tell him how I got bitten and sipping on a drink while I did so.

Or the time that the cat wouldn't eat and I thought he knew he was dying and was trying to tell us so. The truth was my spoiled Jewish cat got a taste of turkey and canned food and refused to eat food that was "below" him. I really thought he was dying and actually lost sleep because he knew and couldn't tell us.

There's tons more where this came from. I'm compiling some of the best for a future blog post. This was just the teaser. I hope you'll come back and read more soon.

* * * * * * * * * * * * * * * * * * *

The Origins Of Worry

When I reread the previous section about not sweating the small stuff and worry that many of you may think I am certifiably crazy. I'm not. In fact, I live a wildly productive and happy life in spite of being mildly (ok severely) phobic. My husband loves me just as I am. My friends indulge my neuroses not because they have to but because they actually accept me for me. My dog is more faithful that Lassie (and while she cannot rescue a small animal or child stranded in a deep well, she's pretty exceptional.) The list goes on. I'm lucky. Happy and lucky. Period.

Ironically, I worried about this for days until I finally said fuck it, I don't really care what you think. I don't know you. You don't know me. We could meet in the street today and you won't be like, "Hey, it's that crazy Mindy lady from the blog. She's batshit crazy and it shows!" Just kidding- I'm not that mean. I kind of do care what you think but it won't define me- fair?

The post did, however, give me pause for thought. Why am I this way? How is it that others can get through a day without worrying that their aspirin is tainted, that the oxygen is properly flowing on their airplane (before, during and after takeoff) that there is no streaking around that mosquito bite that could lead to Red Nile Virus or malaria or whatever the "bad" kind of mosquito can do to you?

And I found some answers! I take responsibility for a small part of my eccentricity- I was either born with it or created it. The rest, well there are a lot of fingers to point here friends (yes, I just said I didn't give a flip what you thought of me and now I call you friends... duplicitous to the max today, I am!)

Here is the conclusion I've arrived at. There were a series of events in my life, starting very early on, that triggered the perpetual Mindy worry-fest. By way of example, consider these:

Pepsi- It's Pepsi's Fault

When we were little our family's soda of choice was Pepsi. We grew up in Boston where Coke was frowned upon. The only relevancy here is that Pepsi is a drink that I frequently fetched from the fridge for Sarah.

"Min, go get me a soda." Panting puppy dog (ie little sister) runs down to the kitchen and gets her big sis a drink. Then we happily played with our Barbies and their cool dune buggies. Life was good. Sarah is 14 months older than I am- she was my idol.

Then Sarah proposed a trade. My very cool green dune buggy with the flower decals for... a jack. Yes, one jack. I gave her a wind up dune buggy and she gave me one jack. No ball. Not the other nine needed for a game. One jack. But I was in heaven. She was playing with me, paying attention to ME! Man was I lucky to have her for a sister.

So later I said, "Hey, Sarah. Go get me a Pepsi." When she recovered from her uncontrollable laughter she simply uttered, "No." The 6 year old equivalent of go fuck yourself.

Lesson learned. It was the last Pepsi this dune buggyless, one jack five year old ever got her.

The Mommom Name Change Conspiracy Theory:

Sarah and I referred to our grandmother as "Mommom" for as long as I can remember. Our first cousins called her Bubbe. Ok, potAto, potAHto, right? Wrong. One day when I was about fourteen I heard Sarah refer to "Mommom" as "Bubbe." WTF? Who changed the game and why wasn't I invited?

Then it struck me. Sarah went to Florida with our cousins Miriam and Michaela (yes, my family has issues with names that start with "M") and stayed with Mommom and Papa for a week. \ When she returned, BAM, it was Bubbe. This was a devastating blow from which I have likely never recovered.

A Bat-Mizvah Mishap

Yes, there are a bazillion photos of the candle-lighting ceremony from my bat-mitzvah (October 1978.) What's the problem you ask? What's missing in all of the photos? ME. Freakin' ME! They forgot to call me up for my own candle-lighting ceremony.

Sarah and my best friend Maddie (another "M") did a fab job rolling out my cake. Mommom (yes, "Mommom", not "Bubbe" because I am still not a member of that club) and Papa on both sides, Mom and Dad, close friends…. All got to light candles. Mindy- beige Mindy who must just blend into the woodwork- didn't light a single candle. In fact, there is no PROOF that I was even there!

I did get lots of checks and can still sing my haftorah so I know I was there, but the pics certainly don't reflect my presence. It was too early for DNA proof so I am left with my memories. And the worry that my bat mitzvah and 9 years of Hebrew school are a gross figment of my imagination, a distortion of reality.

Last, but not least….

Garbage Grief

So my parents got relocated to Atlanta for my dad's job. We were in college but home for the summer when they were set to move. The house in Atlanta wasn't ready so we were put up in a very nice high rise apartment. Because we were on the 20th floor, there was a garbage chute that went to the basement garbage collection area.

One day Sarah was at work when she realized she threw away her gold and diamond rings- two of them. Yes, she threw them away. Don't ask. This shit just seems to happen to Sarah.

Anyway, she calls me from work hysterical and says, "You have to go find them. Mom is going to kill me." (Aside- I stopped short of asking if she had a special nickname for Mom that I wasn't privy to, frankly, because like in the film "A Few Good Men", I couldn't 'handle the truth' after the Mommom-Bubbe thing.)

Anyway, not only am I a worrier, I am a pleaser. So I marched down to the basement floor of the building and found the facilities office. The manager walked me into the most disgusting, repulsive, putrid-smelling, fetid, filthy room I have ever seen. There were hundreds of bags of trash piled ten feet high. Fortunately, germ phobia is not on Mindy's roster of fears so in I went!

OCD (obsessive compulsive disorder) is also one disorder I skirted. My mother, on the other hand, was and is an OCD maven. The disorder that drove my mom to superhero magnitudes of consistency and order saved Sarah's sorry ass. Mom bought only one kind of garbage bag. Ever. White plastic with bright pink handle ties.

Like an oasis in the desert, through the hideous array of refuse and rubbish, there they were. Two shiny white bags with bright pink handle ties. I walked right over to them, opened one up and began the fishing expedition through food, paper, snot rags and G-d knows what else. I hit gold on the first try. There, wrapped in a paper towel, were Sarah's two rings.

I gave the facilities guy twenty bucks and ran back upstairs to phone Sarah. She was over the top, thankful and appreciative. I felt great.

Then she laughed. And laughed. And laughed some more. What was so funny, I wanted to know. She happily shared that she would never had touched that putrid pile of shit if it had been my rings. Memories of dune buggies and jacks game flooding back in. The room was spinning. 19 years old and I realized that being the pleaser was my destiny.

Pleaser and worrier. That's me. And I'm okay with it.

Oh, and I get to write this awesome book about all the crazy, wonderful people in my life. So I guess we're even. And I'm happy.

****

Now that I've cracked the code on WHY I am the way I am, it's a lot easier to share a few more embarrassing circumstances in which panic prevailed. After all, I have some to blame now.

A False Alarm

"Attention, attention. The fire alarm was inadvertently sounded, please return to your offices." This is what I heard at 2:45pm on an otherwise quiet Wednesday afternoon at work, when the alarm did in fact go off. Okay, fair enough. Someone tripped it in error. Back to prepping for my 3pm call.

Buzzzzzzzzzzzzzzzzz. "The emergency on the 24th floor has been contained." Buzzzzzzzzzzz. "We repeat, the crisis has been contained."

OK, I know my thought process is not always rational, but my internal alarm began to sound in unison with the unremitting buzz of the building's alert system.

I calmly walked out of my office to find all of my colleagues going about business as usual. It was as if they didn't hear the piercing shrill of the still sounding fire alarm. Apparently they were satisfied with the contained crisis pronouncement and disinclined to even question the nature of the emergency.

I, on the other hand, was than delighted to know there was a crisis requiring suppression in the first place. And the fact that the alarm continued to sound did not bolster confidence that emergency was in fact over.

"Hey guys, do you hear the alarm?"

"Yeah. False alarm."

"Hmmm. Ok. Yeah, but why does it continue to sound?" As calmly as I could muster, "And what do you think the, uh, crisis, was on the 24th floor?"

"No clue." And back to calls, proposals, meetings they went.

My inside voice was screaming "What the fuck is wrong with you people??? Haven't you see 'The Towering Inferno?' There is a *crisis* on the 24th floor, the alarm is sounding and you act like you are exempt from becoming tomorrow morning's CNN Headline News."

My outside persona simply walked to the employee entrance to verify no-one had locked it from the outside, rendering us helpless victims of this horrific terror plot. The door swung wide open. Phew.

I strode coolly back to my office to ensure the phones were working. Nope. Lights blinking like a circuit had been broken. Not good. We WERE hostages. Oh my G-d we need to get out. NOW.

We are on the tenth floor of this midtown structure surrounded by parking decks, businesses and sidewalks. All made of cement. You see where I'm going? It was looking like we might need to crash one of the building's quadruple reinforced industrial grade glass panes. But then

39

what? Where would we go? It was a modern day tower of terror, 40 years after the original hit the big screen. I was sure. All we were missing was Paul Newman and Steve McQueen. I did not want to die here.

Then a funny thing happened.   The alarm stopped. The phones went back on. People were using *the elevators.* A sure sign we were ok. Everyone knows to use the stairs in time of danger. We made it!

Now 2:59pm. Still time to make my call. What felt like hours actually transpired in a matter of minutes. Hopefully, that's all this harrowing experience shaved off my life.

Chapter Five

Family Travel

Family, as defined by Webster's Dictionary, is "the basic unit in society traditionally consisting of two parents rearing their children." What Mr. Webster neglects to address in that definition is that the "basic unit" is comprised of widely varying personalities, views and inclinations which results in a host of fascinating daily interactions. Most families tolerate these disparities, at least to some extent, to keep cohabitation peaceful for the time that the unit is obliged to share a roof.

What I noticed when our family would depart our split level suburban home was an exacerbation of bad behaviors normally kept in check. Honestly, it was like releasing a caged animal into the wild. Upon release from captivity, the Levy clan went from a seemingly happy, normal family to four rabid creatures competing for the same prey. Bad manners, insults, you name it. It was just weird.

Later in life, when we all had our own homes and lives, it got even worse. I guess the years and freedom to form independent habit, routine and opinion become ingrained. And hard to change, even temporarily when the "unit" comes back together.

Living Levy- Travel Tips (of what NOT to do....)

Have you seen the movie "Up in the Air?" This isn't that.

My family has logged thousands of air miles between us. Dad commuted weekly from Boston to Toronto when I was a teen. We now realize that he was far too happy on Sunday nights before he left us in the dust for an estrogen-free, dramaless hotel room. I guess living with three women can take its toll. We know he loved us because he gave the gig up after 2 years. Of course, Sarah and I were in college by then. Hmmmm.

I had a sporadic, irrational fear of flying (funny now that I'm on planes every month) that popped up at very inconvenient moments. Like the time I flew to visit friends for the weekend on Dad's frequent flyer miles. Trip there- easy breezy. Unfortunately, a sense of doom and dread cropped up just before I was boarding the plane home. My dad's best friend had taken me to the airport and looked truly stunned when I said, "I'm not going. The plane is going to crash." No reason, just because.

What does one do with a 19 year old who won't fly "just because?" One calls MOM (not Dad) who calls Dad. It was like a Christmas miracle. Three hours later my Dad appeared at the gate from which I was supposed to depart. He found me looking pathetic and embarrassed. He kicked my ass for making him leave work (where, by the way, he ran the entire company so it was no easy task) and rescue his anxiety-ridden kid, right? WRONG. He gave me a hug, rebooked my ticket and took me home. Maybe because Mom made him, maybe because he's amazing or maybe both. Either way, I could have been shattered by the experience but my parents came through. Like always.

Back to the family flying thing. Not a la George Cluny.

My sister seemed to think she was the ONLY one who was cramped, uncomfortable and mistreated during air travel (thankfully, air marshals were more tolerant of "edgy" passengers back then) and Mom was an Afrin sniffing, overall poor flyer. So, flying with the Levy's as a family was no treat.

Voila. You now have context. Here are some anecdotes from our family travel escapades then and now.

****

On The Road Again (to college)

A successful high school senior, I applied to several schools not in my native Massachusetts, but in surrounding states. Fortunately, I was accepted to all of them. Sara was already a flourishing freshman at UMASS, about 90 minutes from home. I wanted to go a little bit further, but not too far from home. I actually liked my parents and wanted to be able to come home to visit often.

One fine Spring day, Mom, Dad and I loaded up the family sedan and set course for Syracuse University in upstate New York. I was psyched. The school looked soooo cool. It met all my criteria for a college: Big, citylike and a community of 15,000 students. Yay. From there we planned to visit Ithaca College, a short 56 miles away.

We made the six hour trek talking, laughing and with great anticipation of the magical welcome we'd receive as we approached the gates of this great institution. 10 minutes to go, almost there!

"Welcome to Syracuse". No, that was not a sign on any ivy laden, gold plated gates. It was me. Yes, with just a touch of sarcasm and disappointment, I uttered those words from the back seat, just loud enough for my parents to glean in the front seat.

There was no definitive landmark or crested arch with the school's insignia to signal we were now on university property. It was kind of dumpy, actually. I didn't know much, but I did know that I was NOT going to school here. It just felt... icky.

Dad was about to park the car so we could get out and have a walk around campus. I reaaallllly didn't want to. This place was dreary, ugly and no place for a vibrant young mind like mine. I tried. I really tried to tow the line and at least have a look. But alas, the stubborn 6 year old that used to drive my dad nuts re-emerged, and out it came.

"I'm not going here. I don't like it."

Dad: "Excuse me?"

Oh shit, it was the same look I got when I was on the magic stairs (the escalator) at Filene's when I was five years old. Dad had told me not to walk up the down escalator. I did it anyway. I got stuck. Up and down. Up and down. But I wasn't going anywhere. Just stuck in the middle of that steep electronic staircase.

I couldn't tell if he was pissed or worried, probably both. Anyway, I passed him a couple of times as he tried to go up and retrieve me from the top, then finally boarded the down escalator to whisk me off to safety. I was laughing and giddy- it was soo much fun. And the grand finale was riding the escalator with no feet or hands- just in Daddy's arms. It was heaven.

"Wipe that smile off your face young lady." Huh? Daddyies didn't say that in heaven. Was he serious? We were having such a ball together. Nah, I must have misheard. Back with an even bigger grin, my Daddy was the best, most fun dad in the world.

What's that? At the bottom of the escalator was six year old Sara. Also grinning. But wait, she wasn't on the escalator having fun with us. So why was she smiling? Then it hit me. She knew. It was an ominous, creepy grin. She was taking pleasure in my ignorance of the reality that any worry my dad felt had turned to outright anger. He was fuming.

Same look as right now from the front seat of our Oldsmobile sedan.

"Get out. I didn't drive six fucking hours for you to not look at this school. You did your research and said this was your top choice. You WILL look at the school."

I'm no dummy (well, at least I don't make the same mistake twice.) I got out. I looked. I made benign comments, even complimented a few things about the campus. Departure from the dog house almost complete.

We return to the car and get in. Mom and Dad asked what I thought and I said I really didn't think it was for me. It was too big, citylike and the community of 15,000 students was daunting. Time to change my selection criteria, but I had hoped they wouldn't notice.

Off to Ithaca we went.

We arrived in Ithaca, a quaint little town with both the esteemed Cornell University and smaller Ithaca College campuses right next to one another. It was beautiful. The grounds were perfectly manicured, the campus navigable and accessible.

"I'll go here."

This time Mom. "Excuse me?"

"I'll go here. I like it."

Mom: "Get out of the car." For an instant, she looked just the female version of my dad. Her face actually became his just framed with longer hair and some lipstick. Ewwww.

Suffice it to say that I spent half a day there meeting with students and enrollment advisors, walking the campus and shopping at the bookstore. Mom and dad had formed some bizarre alliance of which I was not a part. They became one, like a two headed monster in the old Creature Features, reigning terror on this unassuming tiny mortal.

I spent four happy years at Ithaca College. I earned my BS in Business, was conversational in French and returned came home to proud parents. Until I showed off my shiny new backpack and announced I was off to backpack through Europe for six months.

****

The Family That Flies Together….

Family trip circa 1988:

Flight Attendant to Dad: "Sir, is the woman in front of you with the Sony Walkman (music blaring out of the headphones) annoying you?"

Dad to Flight Attendant: "She's been annoying me for 22 years. If you can get her to stop now, I'll give you $100."

45

The woman in front? My sister.

The four of us had many adventures together. Trips to Cape Cod, weddings, funerals, vacations. Countless memories. I'm happy to say that we still have family outings but they're now just Sara, Mom and I. We miss Dad every day, but he is with us in spirit on every trip.

* * * * * * * * * * * * * * * * * * *

Things have changed quite a bit since that 1988 trip. Mom, Sara and I are as close as ever. I have two kids of my own, a busy career, great husband, and awesome in-laws. Life is good.

Travel is a different ball game when you go from child to parent, from passenger to pilot if you will. I am the primary orchestrator of our family expeditions. Whether it's camping or a trip to the beach, overseas or a roadtrip to visit family, we love getting away together. The kids are 14 and 17 now so I hope we continue the Levy Legacy of family frolics my parents started with us.

Being a step-mom is one of the biggest joys in my life. I've been with the girls since they were very young and got a very quick initiation into parenthood. I think some of these early escapades helped seal the bond between us. Seriously, you know you have truly bonded with a child when they projectile barf on you across the car somewhere in the middle of G-d's country, and all you feel is love for the little diarrhea plagued babe. Yes, that's love. It's on that foundation, with the knowledge that anything goes when families travel together, that we set out on many an excursion.

Rest Stop Reflections

To the weary traveler, a rest stop offers a welcome break on the long road between home and destination. Twice a year we would drive eight hours with the girls to spend a week with my in-laws. I'm not one for long, boring drives but these trips were different. We never, ever installed a dvd or video player in the car. Instead we played games, talked, listened to music. We learned more about each other in the span of eight hours than most families do over months.

The very first trip I took with Kevin and the girls was in the summer. The girls were about 4 and 7. I remember because I had to wash the barf off Melissa's leggings, size 4T, out of her Barbie's hair and off the BACK of my shirt (I said projectile, didn't I?) in the bathroom of a gas station not 50 miles out of town. We didn't' get very far before the Dunkin Donuts we had for breakfast made a second appearance.

Off we went. It was a great week. We ate yummy food, played board games with Gramma and Papa, went to the drive in and more. How lucky I felt to have such a wonderful extended family.

About five hours into the return trip we decided to switch drivers and stop for dinner. There was a cool sit down restaurant, combined with convenient store and gas station, that looked perfect. As a new stepparent I had quickly learned that I would never pee alone again. Not sure why, but the girls always came with me or just wanted to join me to chat. I wondered if this was normal and at what age it would cease. I'm happy to report that we all pee alone today and have done so for a long time now.

Anyway, we stop at the restaurant and I ask the girls if anyone needs to go potty. No on both fronts. Great, I get to go solo. I announce I'm heading for the rest room and I hear two little voices, in concert, say they need to go, too. Off we went.

"Now girls, I really have to go so we can all go into the handicapped stall together but you'll need to wait with me."

"Okay!"

We get in the stall and no sooner do I sit down then they start asking when I'll be done and that it stinks in there. Oh jeez, it'll just be easier to bring them back to Kevin and come back.

"Girls, I'm going to bring you back to Daddy at the table and I'll come back and finish by myself."

"Okay, let's go!"

No sooner do we emerge from the ladies room, three happy souls, hand in hand, when they spot Kevin 30 feet away at our table. Out of this tiny seven year old comes a bellow that that rivals the most accomplished professional boxing announcer:

"Daddy!!! Mindy had to POOP and it SMELLED really bad so she is bringing us back to the table now. She will go back to the bathroom without us and finish POOPING alone."

Oh. My. G-d. Every patron in the restaurant, in the thirty foot expanse that separated me from my beloved and beyond, was staring at me. Some were laughing. Some just felt bad. Others had to look away for fear of locking eyes with me. Anna was beaming- she had no clue that any normal adult would have been mortified at having their most private bodily necessity revealed to a restaurant full of strangers.

Fortunately, I am not your normal adult and have little to no angst about how the general public perceives me. What you see if what you get. I proceeded to say hello to a few my fellow diners, now acquaintances of a kind, on the way to deliver my little darlings to their dad.

I returned to the ladies room only to discover a long piece of toilet paper stuck to my shoe. Yes, it was there for the round trip voyage to and from the table. It only added to the humor of the situation.

We tell that story often, and have a good chuckle again and again. And I thank Melissa and Anna for reinforcing my ability to survive public humiliation with grace and dignity.

****

Birds of a Feather

This particular snippet is the result of a recent mother-daughter trip to Florida where I was nearly taken out by a headless driver (old people are *very* short) in the Publix parking lot, berated by an enima wielding elderly patron in CVS, and witness to a "hit and I just don't care that I hit you because you are going to die soon anyway" car wreck at the local flee market.

Entry filed in: *Retirement, Money, Worry*

Gotta earn money, then spend money to retire, right? Wrong. After (very little) reflection, it's safe to say that, with Jewish people, money and everything go hand in hand so let's talk retirement and be on the alert for the money theme here. You won't have to work very hard.

After a long career, my mom retired from her executive role in HR and decided to build a second home in Florida for the winter months. She is officially a "snowbird" now. Cool! Every six months I fly down with her to get her moved in then perform the opposite exercise to come back home.

After my first trip to Boynton Beach, I began to wonder if it was mandatory for every Jew east of the Mississippi and north of the Mason Dixon line to relocate to Florida upon retirement. I wondered if I would end up like the stereotypical old Jewish people we used to laugh about. You know, the ones who take sugar packets and mints from restaurants, loiter in the supermarket deli section for more free samples, wear socks and sandals on the beach, and carry out a variety of miserly, money-related exploits that undermine the small percentage of us who are willing to buy our own sugar, go barefoot and pay fair price.

This has gone from a topic I ponder to a gripping, almost paralyzing fear. I am 46 years old. How much time do I have left? Is a car going to show up at my house when I turn sixty and whisk me away to Del Boca Vista where the Seinfeld's lived? Maybe I'll get a pass because I married a goy.

I don't know but these thoughts are not good for one with a natural predisposition to anxiety and apprehension. If I only have 14 years until I morph into a condiment pilfering meshuggeneh, just shoot me now. I do

NOT want to turn into one of those old tightwads that turns parting with a dollar to a complex hostage negotiation. I've seen it folks, it's not pretty.

Back to Boynton

My sister, Sarah, lives in California. Recently she decided to plan a trip to Florida to visit my mom and asked if I wanted to meet her there. I told her yes, but then my travel schedule for work became pretty hectic so in the end I couldn't swing it.

Or could I?

I gave her a definitive "no" and immediately called Mom to tell her the ruse was on! I booked my flight and held my breath that neither Mom nor I would blow it the three weeks between that call with Sarah and the surprise weekend.

Being the incredibly rule-bound person I am, trying to maintain a lie in any form (even for something fun like this) is a challenge and very stressful. I just don't like it and pretty much suck at it.

Being the incredibly rule-averse person my mother is, trying to maintain a lie in any form is not at all stressful, just confusing. So many details to remember (did I say *this* or did I say *that*?) In fact, she pulled the wool over my dad's eyes every five years with surprise birthday parties and he never, ever knew. That says either my mom was incredibly sly or my dad was incredibly oblivious. I think I know the truth but opt for a compromise rather than concede that my dad was c-l-u-e-l-e-s-s! Adorable, but clueless.

Anyway, not gifted in the area of masking irritation, Sarah kind of brushed me off when I told her my business trip was canceled but I wasn't coming to Florida anyway. I got it, though. She was introducing her new beau to Mom and friends for the first time and wanted me to meet him, too. It was all I could do not to tell her I was coming.

Suffice it to say, she was very surprised to find me at Mom's on her return from the obligatory "I've arrived in Florida and survived the Publix parking lot" supermarket run."

Do you remember the limerick I wrote about food? I had so much fun that I've written another to sum up our fab weekend together.

My sister and Mom got together
To enjoy the warm Florida weather
I said I was booked
But that was a hook
We ate our way through two days together

In the last chapter, I share more on words of wisdom and lessons from my days in Boynton. This little snippet is just to whet your appetite (sorry, the food thing is pervasive....)

Trapezoid: the chemical in turkey that makes you tired after you eat it. (Oh, also a quadrilateral with two sides parallel, but who knew?)

Confirmed: Food is king. All meals discussed, planned and agreed for an entire 72 hour timeframe. Dinner successfully executed, onto breakfast.

No-one can finish a fucking sentence around here. I consider myself pretty sharp but can't follow a single thread of conversation because no sentence gets completed. I'm Jewish and should really excel here but think I've been weakened as a result of my non-Jewish husband and extended family. On reflection, this is a good thing. These people must walk around exhausted all the time trying to catch up with themselves.

Loud. You must be loud or you're toast.

****

She Wore An Isty Bitsy Teenie Weenie Cotton Underwear Bikini

Las Vegas. Lights, casinos, food , shows. Some of the world's best performers appear in her grand theaters these days. It's even referred to

51

as the entertainment capital of the world. Mom and I love Las Vegas. We discovered this mutual adoration for the city of lights quite by accident when we decided to have a girls' weekend there several years back. Nothing like bonding with Mom over a penny slot machine!

Las Vegas. Trade shows, work, business dinners. That was the basis for my most recent trip out West. I hadn't had a vacation in some time so I asked Kevin if he wanted to come with me and spend a couple of days relaxing before my meetings started. We booked our tickets and looked forward to two days and nights of fun before I had to don geek attire and my conference badge.

We arrived early evening and had a splendid dinner. Off to the casino for a little play and a romantic night alone together. Ahhhh, it felt good to kick back and unwind.

Just before I fell asleep I spied my open suitcase, on top of which sat my business clothes. A touch of distraction as I remembered the presentations I was to give just 36 hours from now. Oh, and I hope everything is ok back home. Did we leave enough food for the dog and cat? I finally fell asleep, a less zen than an hour earlier.

We woke up and ordered room service. It was grand- heaps of good food and even better coffee. This was the life! No dog to walk, no kids to drive to school, just me and my number one guy!

Bzzzz. What's that? It's Sunday. Who's calling us when we are officially OFF THE GRID? It was my iPhone, my work phone. I did not answer, didn't even look. I had 24 more hours of perfect serenity with my man and I was going to relish every second.

Da-ding. A text message. Now it must be really important for someone to text me on a Saturday, knowing I was out of town and out of the office through the following Tuesday. So I looked. "Did you get that Latin America deal in yet?" Really? Reaaallly? I'm not sure if I was more upset with my boss for intruding on my weekend or at myself for reading the text. Grrr. Shake it off, Mindy.

We finished our breakfast and decided to head to one of the hotel's magnificent pools. The weather was perfect- 80 degrees, sunny, slight breeze. We changed into our suits and were just about ready to leave when I decided to make a pit stop in the bathroom. All set, sunglasses in hand, we made our way to the pool.

We found some lounge chairs in a perfect spot- part sun, part shade. Refreshments were in order. I had chosen one of my fab Title Nine bikini's and thought I'd look cooler walking to the bar, which was quite a distance away, in my denim shorts with the vibrant colored top. We were definitely two of the more hip people staying at Aria, if I do say so myself. Both pretty fit, designer shades and no ink. I felt good. Really good. I could just feel the relaxation pouring back into my weary brain and body.

I handed Kevin the drinks and took my shorts off poolside. iPad in one hand, drink in the other, I cozied up on my lounge and began to read. We were a bit crammed because the lounge chairs all nearly touched one another. The lady on my right was kind of glaring at me and appeared wound pretty tight. I felt bad for her- here we were in this beautiful place and all she could do was stare at me with pursed lips, probably because her life sucked so badly and Kevin and I were so at ease. Maybe marital problems, maybe worse. Who knew.

Fifteen minutes later I put my iPad down and planned to nap. Sleep never came. When I looked down I did not see the adorable, perfectly sculpted bottom to my fab Title Nine bikini. What I saw was a plain, flesh colored pair of cotton underwear- the equivalent of "*tighty*-whiteys" on a man! Oh my f-ing G-d. I never put on the bottoms! How could this be.

I leaped to my feet like a high jump vaulter in the Olympics. Those shorts were on in milliseconds.

I look at Kevin and say "holy shit, I am in my underwear!" He says, "yeah, I know."

Yeah, I know???? Yeah, I know????

"If you knew, then why didn't you say something when you saw me take off my shorts?? I've been sitting by the pool in my freakin' underwear for fifteen minutes!"

"I wasn't sure if you meant to do it. I thought maybe it was a mix and match bathing suit or something."

Who is this man and where the hell is my husband? The one who has seen my underwear a million times and should really be able to identify it in any lineup, any day.
"Great. Well if I show up to dinner in a skirt and bra, please do let me know BEFORE we are seated."
Odd

I recovered from the incident but only after hours of brooding whether this was the beginning of early onset Alzheimer's. I was really worried that I was losing it. In the end, we figured out I was doing too many things at once, like always, and brought my suit bottom to the rest room before we left for the pool. Right where I found it, on the sink, when we returned.

****

Chapter Six

Illness, Funerals and Money

What's Ailing You?

Everyone handles illness differently. Remember when Kevin had surgery and didn't bother to tell his parents? When he is sick, whether it's a cold or full blow flu, he just takes it in stride and tries to shake it off.

Me, too. In another world where unicorns fly.

I am a maniac when I'm sick. I hate it. There is no time to be sick, I have too much to do! Oh, and it scares the shit out of me.

I'm great when someone else is sick. Like the time Mom had a horrible allergic reaction to a medication and ignored the doctor's order to take a steroid to combat it. Two weeks of back and forth to her house, home health IV infusions and an increasingly nasty attitude toward me and the world in general. Yes, I handled that like a champ. When she told me that if I put her in the hospital she "didn't care if she ever came out" I quickly told her to fuck off and called 911.

Then there was the time that Kevin choked on a piece of chicken. Technically, he was breathing because little bits of air could get down his windpipe. The fact that no saliva or molecule of additional oxygen could make it's way past his tonsils didn't seem to matter to him. He jumped from stair to stair convinced he could dislodge it. I kept my cool. For the first two hours. After that, I hauled his ass to the emergency room (the same one, by the way, that Mom ended up at following the 911 call.)

I was worried (there's a shocker) that the choking was a complication from his newly diagnosed MS. After a few hours, the GI specialist that was called in came out to see me in the waiting room. I anxiously asked if this was caused by MS and if we need to find an aggressive form of treatment to make sure it didn't happen again.

"Your husband need to chew. I pulled out a giant hunk of chicken from his esophagus."

Touche. Suffice it to say, Kevin would have been better off if it had been the MS. Who eats a 3 inch chunk of chicken? Ever heard of a knife, Einstein?

****

Anyway- I can make fun of others all day long. This is classic Mindy.

"You can get lost on the way to the hospital to treat the illness you don't have."

This was my husband's statement to me as I was walking my directionally challenged ass out to a business meeting while obsessing about the strange bite on my arm. It's definitely not a mosquito bite, but likely not the deadly recluse spider bite that I'm convinced will turn into a flesh eating bacterial infection.

Those of you have read previous posts know I am a hypochondriac, no surprise there. But this time I am basking in sweet vindication. Just back from the doctor who put me on an antibiotic for this very *REAL* spider bite. Admittedly, this is a bit of a twisted triumph. I mean who celebrates a bug bite? Apparently me. Whatever, I am celebrating that I am not crazy and had the good sense to get this checked out.

And I did **NOT** get lost on the way to the doctor.

My time in the waiting room gave me an opportunity to reflect on the different ways people handle illness. For example, when Kevin and I were still dating he had to have outpatient surgery. So I took the day off work, drove him to the hospital and stayed with him until he was up and about again the next day. Normal, right? Right.

What I found incredibly abnormal was that when I called him mom to let her know everything went well, she asked, "Everything what went well?" Really? Really, Kevin??? While this was not major surgery it did involve a scalpel, anesthesia and a release form signature stating that neither the hospital nor any of their employees were liable should you kick off during this very routine procedure.

This is an extreme departure from how my family rolls. I suspect it's part of the contrast between Jewish and non-Jewish cultures. I get a hangnail and the entire East Coast is mobilized:

> Mom: "Marsha, Mindy has hangnail. No, no, it's not infected. Yet. Oy, what if it becomes infected?"

> Marsha: "Hello Sandy, Blanche just phoned. Mindy has a hangnail. Infected? Maybe, I can't remember. OH VEZ MEAR, why can't I remember? Let's conference in Marilyn, she'll know.

> "Hello Marilyn? It's Marsha and Sandy. Did you hear? You DID! So is it infected? You don't think so? From your mouth to G-d's ears."

> And so on. Think I'm kidding? I'm not.

Anyway, now that Kevin and I have been married for a long time we have a good balance of when to alert the family and when it's better to just keep quiet. Somewhere between my apprehension and his unbelievably maddening calmness is a happy medium.

****

Illness Induced Stress

They say the stress of illness or death brings out the worst in people. They're right. From refusal to take sound medical advice to making a "doggie bag" to go at a funeral, I have seen it all. At first glance, I was quite concerned that most of this misconduct was a direct tie to the Jewish-Worry-Money connection. Honestly, I have stories that can't be shared here because they so strongly reinforce the stereotype that I'd feel personally responsible for bolstering the bias against my clan.

I experienced a perverse sense of relief as a bystander, non-participant, voyeur to my non-Jewish husband's family pandemonium. No, there was not a hint of guilt inducement. No double entendre declarations. Absent were the woes of enmeshed, complex relationships.

What they DID have was a real life story of a WWII hero, extortion and jealousy. Intriguing, no? And what a relief! Suddenly, my family wreaking havoc in hotels and hair salons didn't seem so extreme. I no longer walk alone on my person path of peculiar. And Jews everywhere can breathe a sigh of relief in the knowledge that everyone is crazy, not just us.

To be fair, or maybe to establish credibility for this rather bold proclamation, imagine yourself driving up to a stately Ohio home on a sunny Saturday afternoon. An "Estate Sale" sign in the front yard reveals that the elderly couple, Kevin's grandparents, have decided to make the transition to a retirement home after decades of memories in this house. His grandfather, a retired two star general, and grandmother had lived there for decades- it was a grueling decision.

Kevin's parents, Carl and Betty, were on hand to help as were Carl's siblings. My in- laws are nothing short of awesome. I can spend hours, days with them and never get tired of them. They are happy, loving, fun people that I am lucky to count as family. It's not their fault that Kevin's aunt Madeline skipped the chapter in the book of happy and loving. Nor do their bear responsibility for her fundamental greed and self-absorption.

What follows is a tale of avarice, ego and insider trading gone bad. They say what goes around comes around. In this case, it does. Literally.

Table Stakes

Back at the estate sale. My father-in-law, Carl, is a real estate agent with lots of experience in this stuff. He is also a loving son who truly cares about his parents. Naturally, he was there at the estate sale to oversee activities and look after his parents' valuables as they went to their new owners.

Unfortunately, Madeline, who lived in the same town, wanted to capitalize on the event. She had her eye on the family dining set and decided she'd take it and sell her own set in its place. She removed the furniture weeks earlier without permission and replaced it with her own. Kind of disgusting if you ask me, but alas, you did not ask.

 And the bidding began. Off went some light fixtures, a desk and various end tables. Carl worked diligently to keep track of everything while Madeline was counting her portion of the proceeds. Oh, wait, what do you mean the proceeds go to Mom and Dad for the assisted living expenses? I'll just take my part, you do what you want with yours.

Me again but, excuse me. What part of they're still ALIVE are you missing??? You don't have a "part", it's THEIRS. Jeez, she could have been Jewish if it weren't for the froo froo clothes and Kentucky Derby style hats she wore.

The table. A few bids, not very high. How could this be? You could see the disbelief on Madeline's taut face. The thought bubble I envision over her head says something like… "My table was custom made of the best materials. Unacceptable. "

Fear not, she had a sure fire plan. Ever hear the term "hedge your bet?" Loosely defined and mostly used in financial circles, it is an attempt protect yourself against a possible loss. Madeline didn't like losses.

Oddly enough, just when they though the table would sell for the low $250 bid that had been made, another came in. This time is was a huge jump to about $900. Wow. Madeline must have been relieved.

But she wasn't. In fact, she was pacing and sweating a little bit. It was weird. A few more rounds of bidding and the auction was over. Finito, and everything had been sold. Even the table for a whopping $900!

But Madeline wasn't happy. In fact, Madeline was pissed. You see, she had anonymously bid the $900 in an effort to drive up the price of the table. She was "hedging her bet." Well folks, when you hedge a bet it is good practice to research the market first. She didn't.

So at the end of the day, Madeline wrote a check for $900 to the third party auction house for HER own table. Then she wrote another check for the transport fee to have it moved back to her home. I never heard about the incident again, nor did Carl and Betty, but I suspect there is a bitter aftertaste at the conclusion of each meal at Madeline's house.

****

For Here Or To Go?

We have a very close knit group of friends who, since I was a child, have vacationed together, celebrated bar-mitvah's then marriages and sadly, the shared loss of loved ones. It's comforting to be surrounded by people who really know you when the going gets tough and that has made such losses a bit more bearable.

But there are always the friends who are just a little bit off. You know, the ones who take food off your plate for a taste without asking (ok for close friends, big no-no for an acquaintance.) Or the pal that thinks your really do want to pay for their popcorn at the movies EVERY time. Then there are the one who outright lie about money with, "Why yes, I did tip the waiter", or "Oh, I forgot my wallet. Again." This latter category of friend is not only annoying but insufferable.

Jewish people are often pigeonholed as cheap. Fair enough, there are plenty of cheap Jews out there. But there are plenty of normal Jews, like my close peeps and family, who spend money like the rest of the world and are quite generous. It is due to that upbringing that I find the popcorn pinching cheapskate who reuses an old bag from the previous movie to secure a free refill repugnant. Seriously, these people have a giant house and drive a BMW. Why the hell do they need to beat the system with a $7 refreshment ruse?

It's like a game to them, or maybe an illness. How much can we get for free? This surpasses the benign condiment pilferer or serial soda refiller. I'm talking about some seriously twisted behavior as evidenced by Bonnie and Jacob after a friend's funeral.

It was a sad day for us all. After the funeral, we all went back to the family home to celebrate the life that was just lost and support our friend who was now a widow. The only thing of greater magnitude than the love that flooded the room was the food that flowed freely and covered every available table or counter surface. Yes, we have already established the significance of food in any Jewish event, happy or sad, birth or death.

People gave hugs as they departed, offered their condolences and promised to stop by often. Bonnie and Jacob were about to take their leave.

"Where's the Tupperware?" Oh, that's really sweet. They were going to help clean up and put the leftovers away.

"In the cabinet over the sink. But it's ok, I can do it later."

"Do it later? Oh, yes, certainly you will. We were just looking for some containers for our food. We thought we'd take some home- the deli and knishes will be great for lunch tomorrow."

No-one spoke. We couldn't. I was about to scream something pretty ugly, I could feel the anger burning up my esophogus. I had lost my dad the month before and knew what an awful, painful time this was for my friend. But something stopped me, I don't know what. It was like the wire to my vocal cords was fried and nothing came out.

Bonnie and Jacob left with their funeral doggie bag. No, they had not contributed to the catering. No, they did not ask if they could help. And yes, they departed as if they had just finished their fortune cookie at the local Chinese restaurant, plastic sac of leftovers in hand.

Ick.

Epilogue

Lessons Learned

This will be a very short chapter. I really haven't learned any lessons. I continue to worry too much and still have that penchant to please. What I have learned is that it's okay. I try not to make the same mistakes twice but can't promise I won't. I will continue to love my family and friends with everything I have. Tomorrow will be full of challenges. I say, bring it. When challenge and adversity hit this family, we tackle it head on a la "Monty Python and the Holy Grail":

"I don't wanna talk to you no more, you empty headed animal food trough wiper! I fart in your general direction! You mother was a hamster and your father smelt of elderberries!"

The End

Made in the USA
Charleston, SC
02 April 2013